GORILLAS

GORILLAS

by Paul Hermann Bürgel and Manfred Hartwig

A Carolrhoda Nature Watch Book

Carolrhoda Books, Inc./Minneapolis

Thanks to Victor Camp, Director, Como Zoo, St. Paul, Minnesota, for his assistance with this book.

MAY 3 1993

This edition first published 1992 by Carolrhoda Books, Inc.
Original edition copyright © 1989 by Kinderbuchverlag Reich Luzern AG, Lucerne, Switzerland, under the title BEI DEN BERGGORILLAS. Translated from the German by Amy Gelman.
Adapted by Carolrhoda Books, Inc.
All additional material supplied for this edition copyright © 1992 by Carolrhoda Books, Inc.

LIBRARY OF CONGRESS CATALOGING-IN-PUBLICATION DATA

Bürgel, Paul Hermann.
    [Bei den Berggorillas. English]
    Gorillas / by Paul Hermann Bürgel and Manfred Hartwig.
       p.   cm.
    Translation of: Bei den Berggorillas.
    "A Carolrhoda nature watch book."
    Summary: Describes the physical characteristics, habitat, and life cycle of the gorilla.
    ISBN 0-87614-758-9
    1. Gorilla—Juvenile literature. [1. Gorilla.] I. Hartwig, Manfred. II. Title.
QL737.P96B8713   1992
599.88'46—dc20   92-56
                                                  CIP
                                                  AC

Manufactured in the United States of America

1 2 3 4 5 6 97 96 95 94 93 92

The continent of Africa is home to many remarkable animals. Some are known for their unusual size, like the enormous elephant or the tall, graceful giraffe. Others are fast runners like the gazelle, or powerful hunters like the lion and leopard. Some African animals, for example, the white rhinoceros, are very rare and little known to people.

Of all the animals of Africa, one of the most remarkable and mysterious is the gorilla. For centuries, humans knew almost nothing about gorillas except for stories and legends. Yet people all over the world were fascinated by the giant animals.

Today, thanks to the work of scientists, we know a great deal about gorillas. Facts have replaced legends, and the truth turns out to be just as fascinating as the stories of the past.

One of the reasons that people are fascinated by gorillas may be the special connection that exists between humans and gorillas. Both belong to the same scientific group of animals. Like people, gorillas are classified as **primates** (PRI-maytz). Monkeys and chimpanzees are other members of this group.

Primates have many different physical features, but they have some important things in common. One is a large brain and often a high degree of intelligence. Other features common to many primates are flexible hands able to hold and grasp things.

Within the group of primates, gorillas are most closely related to chimpanzees, orangutans, and gibbons. All these animals are known as **apes**. Humans are close relatives of the apes, although they are not descended from them, as some people believe. Scientists think that human beings and apes had a common ancestor that lived many millions of years ago.

Two members of the ape family, the gibbon and the orangutan, make their homes in Southeast Asia. These animals are tree dwellers, swinging from branch to branch with their long arms. Chimpanzees and gorillas, the other two apes, live in Africa. They are more at home on the ground than their Asian relatives.

There are three groups of gorillas in Africa. One is the western lowland gorilla, which lives in the dense rain forests of Cameroon, Gabon, and other countries of West Africa. The eastern lowland gorilla makes its home in the forests of Zaire.

Orangutan

Chimpanzee

Pigmy chimpanzee

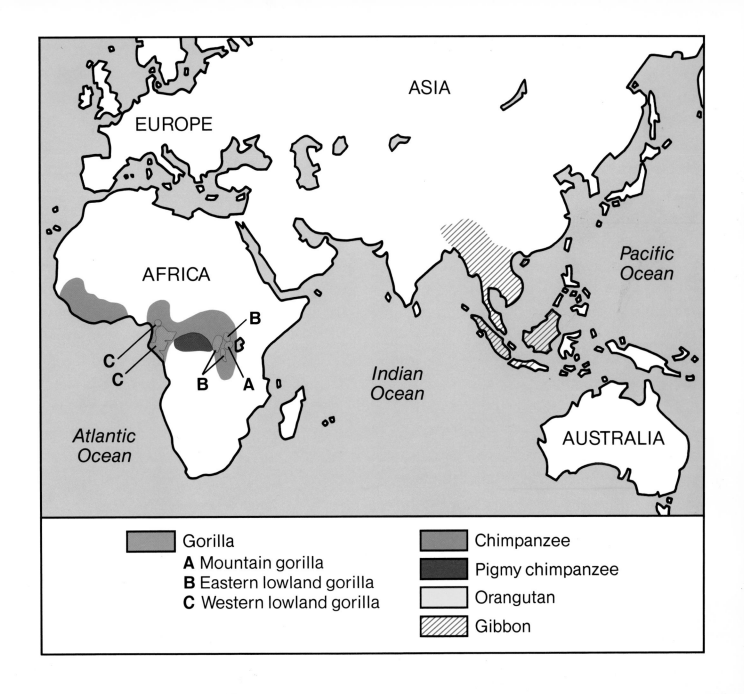

ASIA

EUROPE

AFRICA

B

C
C

B   A

Atlantic
Ocean

Indian
Ocean

Pacific
Ocean

AUSTRALIA

Gorilla
A Mountain gorilla
B Eastern lowland gorilla
C Western lowland gorilla

Chimpanzee
Pigmy chimpanzee
Orangutan
Gibbon

The third kind of gorilla is the mountain gorilla. It also lives in dense rain forests but at much higher altitudes than its lowland relatives. Mountain gorillas are found on the slopes of mountains in the central African countries of Zaire, Rwanda, and Uganda.

Because the mountain gorilla lives in a cold, damp climate, its hair is somewhat longer and thicker than its relatives. But as you can see from the photographs, the three types of gorillas look quite a bit alike.

Western lowland gorilla

Eastern lowland gorilla

All three kinds of gorillas also have very similar ways of living. In this book, we will take a close look at the life and habits of the mountain gorilla.

Mountain gorilla

Mountain gorillas live in cool, humid forests on the slopes of the Virunga Mountains.

The home of the mountain gorilla is a land of mist and rain, of giant trees and tangled green plants. It is located on the slopes of the Virunga Mountains, in central Africa.

The steep Virunga range was formed by the eruption of volcanoes. Today a few volcanoes are still active, but most have been extinct for many years. It is on the slopes of these extinct volcanoes that mountain gorillas live.

The mountain gorilla's home is very near the Equator, in an area where rainfall is heavy. The abundant moisture produces a lush growth of plants. Bamboo flourishes on the lower slopes of the mountains. Higher up, there are thick growths of wild celery, blackberries, and other juicy green plants. Giant moss-covered trees are also common.

Although the Virunga Mountains are near the Equator, the weather there is not hot. The height of the mountains —as much as 14,000 feet (about 4,200 meters)—creates cool, humid days and cold nights. Mountain gorillas need their thick coats of hair to protect them from the chilly temperatures of their homeland.

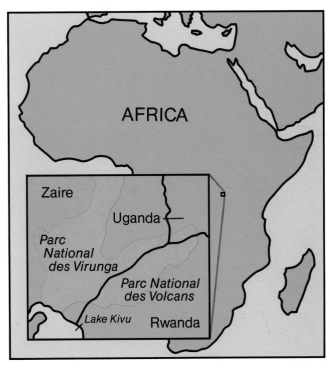

This map shows the national parks established by Zaire and Rwanda to protect mountain gorillas. The parks have French names because this part of Africa was once controlled by Belgium, a European country where French is spoken. The people of Zaire and Rwanda use French as well as their own native languages.

Most of the Virunga range is located in the two African nations of Zaire and Rwanda. Each country has a national park that was created to protect the territory of the mountain gorillas. Let's visit one of these parks to see how the gorillas live today.

Visitors who come to see mountain gorillas have to make their way through the dense forest growth.

Visiting a park where mountain gorillas live is not much like going to Yellowstone or other national parks in the United States. The Virunga Mountains are in the middle of Africa, in an area where transportation can be difficult. Even after visitors arrive at the park, they can't get in a car and drive off to look for gorillas.

The Virunga parks are set up for the protection of mountain gorillas. So there are a lot of rules that human visitors have to follow. For example, only a few people are allowed into a park every day. Each small group of visitors is led by a local guide, a man who knows the park and its gorillas very well. Using this knowledge and his skill as a tracker, the guide will try to locate a group of gorillas.

Following their guide, the visitors slip and slide over the steep, wet forest trails. Sometimes they must fight their way through dense growths of plants. At other times, they have to crawl on their hands and knees. Rain may be pouring down, or the forest may be thick with fog and mist.

The journey is a difficult one, but for most visitors, it is worth it. If they are lucky, the guide finally signals them to stop moving and crouch down. Peering ahead, they see a large, hairy body half hidden among the green plants. A pair of shiny brown eyes looks back at them. They have seen their first mountain gorilla.

Opposite: *Like most primates, mountain gorillas live in groups.* Right: *This gorilla is taking a close look at some human visitors.*

If the visitors see one gorilla, they can be sure that there are other gorillas nearby. Like almost all primates, gorillas are social animals that live in groups. A group of mountain gorillas can have as few as 2 members or as many as 30.

In the national parks of Zaire and Rwanda, there are many different groups of gorillas, some small and some large. Park officials allow people to visit only certain gorilla groups. These groups have become used to having humans near them. The gorillas are not upset if people watch them for several hours or follow them along trails, snapping photos.

Other gorilla groups in the parks are left alone. Although scientists may observe them from time to time, tourists are not permitted to come near them. This system allows some of the mountain gorillas to live a natural life, untouched by human influence.

Even when watching gorillas that are used to people, visitors have to follow strict rules. They must move quietly and stay low to the ground. They have to avoid looking into the eyes of a male gorilla. The animal would see this as a kind of challenge.

The visitors can't touch the gorillas even though the young ones are very curious and sometimes come close. Gorillas get some of the same diseases as humans do, and contact with them could spread disease. In fact, tourists who have colds or other ailments are not even allowed to go into the forest to see the gorillas.

Adult male gorillas are much larger than females. A male can also be recognized by the large crest of hair on the top of his head.

If you were crouched down in the damp forest watching a group of mountain gorillas, what would you see? You would be looking at animals of different sizes and ages. At least one would be a full-grown male gorilla, who would be the leader of the group. There might also be one or two other males that are almost grown.

It is easy to recognize the adult male gorillas in the group. Full-grown males are big! When they stand upright, they may be as much as 6 feet (1.8 meters) tall. They weigh up to 400 pounds (about 180 kilograms) and have very long arms.

The smaller adults in the group are females. Female gorillas weigh about 200 pounds (90 kilograms) and are only about half as tall as the males.

The rest of the group is made up of young gorillas. Some are tiny babies being held in their mothers' arms. Others are lively youngsters running and tumbling around the quiet adults.

A gorilla group is a kind of family, although not all the members are related to each other. The male leader is the head of the family. He plays a very important role in the daily life of the gorilla group.

A young female gorilla

The adult male leader of a gorilla group is called a silverback because of the silvery gray hair on his back. Males develop this light-colored hair when they are about 11 or 12 years old.

The adult male leader of a gorilla group is called a **silverback**. If you look at the photographs on these two pages, you can see why. When a male gorilla is about 11 or 12 years old, the hair on his back starts to turn a silvery color. Female gorillas and young males always have black hair.

As the head of the gorilla group, the silverback has many duties. He leads the group every day as it searches for food in the forest. The silverback also keeps order among the gorillas, preventing them from fighting or quarreling with each other. Finally, he protects the group from danger. He will give up his life if necessary to defend group members from attack.

Along with his duties, the silverback has some privileges. He is the unquestioned leader of the gorilla group. His decisions are final, and all the other gorillas accept them. Perhaps most important, the silverback is the only male in the group that can mate with the females and produce young.

Gorillas in a grove of bamboo plants. Tender bamboo shoots are among the favorite foods of mountain gorillas.

Gorillas usually walk on all fours, with the knuckles of their hands against the ground.

The daily schedule of a mountain gorilla group usually begins when the silverback decides it is time to get up.

The gorillas have slept through the night in **nests** made of plant material. Young gorillas and females may make nests in the lower branches of trees, but the silverback and the other large males always nest on the ground. They are too heavy to climb into trees.

A gorilla nest is not like the complicated structure made by many birds. Instead it consists of branches that are broken off or bent to form a kind of cushion or platform. Each adult gorilla makes its own nest every night, but baby gorillas sleep with their mothers.

When the silverback and the other gorillas roll out of their nests in the morning, the first thing they look for is something to eat. In their forest home, they are surrounded by food. Bark, leaves, shoots, roots, and berries are everywhere. The gorillas may have breakfast at the spot where they spent the night. Or they may start walking slowly through the forest, looking for other food.

The silverback decides which direction to go, and all the other gorillas follow his lead. They move along on all fours, with the knuckles of their hands against the ground. A gorilla can walk on its legs but only for a short distance.

Gorillas eat only plants, and they need a lot of food to keep them going. With their flexible hands, they strip off the outer layers of plants to get to the juicy inner parts. Their powerful teeth cut and grind roots, stalks, and shoots.

A baby gorilla sleeps curled up on its mother's body.

A mountain gorilla group spends the first part of the day eating. About midday, however, it is time for a rest. The silverback picks a spot, and the troop settles down.

The adult gorillas make themselves comfortable on the ground. If it is a sunny day, they may sprawl on their backs, spread out their arms and legs, and take a sunbath. Rain or shine, they will rest or nap for several hours.

Young gorillas don't need as much rest as the adults. The rest period is usually playtime for them. Baby gorillas explore the ground around them, although they never get too far from their mothers. Youngsters of three and four are much more active. They climb trees, wrestle, and chase each other.

In their play, the young gorillas often bump into the resting adults or climb over them. The older gorillas are very patient with the active youngsters. In fact, the big silverback sometimes plays with the young gorillas. He picks them up and **grooms** or tickles them. The youngsters are not at all afraid of their enormous father. They seem to enjoy being near him.

When the silverback decides that the rest period is over, the gorillas move off again to look for food. They may eat for several hours. Then as it begins to get dark, the silverback chooses a place to spend the night. The gorillas make their nests and climb into them. Another day in the forest is over.

This silverback is settling down for his midday nap.

When gorillas nap during the day, they often make nests to sleep in, just as they do at night. These gorillas are all dozing comfortably in their leafy beds.

Young gorillas are a very important part of gorilla life. Like many social animals, gorillas have complicated rules about the way in which their young are born and raised.

One of the rules, as we have seen, is that the silverback is the only male in a group that can have young. He prevents the other adult males from mating with the females. By doing this, the silverback makes sure that all the babies born in the group are his.

In order to reproduce, a young silverback usually has to leave his family group. He wanders in the forest, looking for a lone female to be his mate. Or he finds females willing to leave other groups and join him.

Sometimes a young male on his own tries to take over an existing group and become its leader. To do this, he has to defeat the group's silverback. The competition between the two males does not usually involve a fight. Instead they challenge each other with sounds and movements.

With their hair bristling, the two gorillas exchange stares. Then suddenly, they run toward each other, pounding their chests with their cupped hands. They accompany this booming sound with loud roars. As part of the display, they may also tear off tree branches and wave them or throw them around.

After such a show of strength and fierceness, one of the rivals usually gives up and goes away. If this doesn't happen, then the two males will fight for control of the group. One may be seriously injured or even killed before the conflict is over.

Once a male has collected a group of females, he can mate with them and start a family.

This female gorilla is pregnant and will give birth in a few months.

Left: *A pregnant female gorilla in a zoo.* Opposite: *When a baby gorilla is born, it has very little hair. It depends on its mother for warmth.*

A female gorilla usually has only one baby at a time. She carries it inside her body for eight and a half to nine months. When the baby gorilla is born, it is almost as helpless as a human baby. It needs a lot of care and attention.

In the photograph on the opposite page, you can see a baby gorilla that is only a few days old. This picture and the ones on the next few pages were taken in a zoo. It is very difficult to follow the development of a young gorilla in the wild. The baby in these pictures is a lowland gorilla, but its growth is just like that of its mountain gorilla cousin.

As you can see, a baby gorilla is born with very little hair. The mother keeps the youngster warm by holding it close to her body. Another important thing that the baby needs is food, and the mother provides this as well.

Like all primates, gorillas are **mammals**. A female gorilla feeds her young with milk produced by her body. Held in its mother's arms, the baby nurses frequently during the first weeks of its life.

Held in its mother's arms, a baby gorilla nurses. The youngster will drink its mother's milk until it is about three years old.

Compared to young humans, baby gorillas develop rapidly. They can crawl when they are about three months old. By the time they are five months old, they are able to walk.

But a young gorilla doesn't usually go very far away from its mother. When she moves around, it rides on her back, clinging to her long hair. The baby sleeps cuddled close to its mother. The young gorilla will not be ready to leave her side until it is almost three years old.

During the first few weeks of its life, a baby gorilla has to be introduced to the other members of its group. The birth of a baby is an important event in a gorilla group, whether the gorillas lives in the forest or in a zoo. All the group members are very interested in the newcomer. They gather around the baby, peering at it and reaching out to touch the small furry body. But the mother does not allow the adults or the young gorillas to get too close to her baby. She is very protective of the tiny creature.

Above: *An adult gorilla is very curious about the newest member of the group.*
Opposite: *After meeting relatives for the first time, the baby and its mother take a nap.*

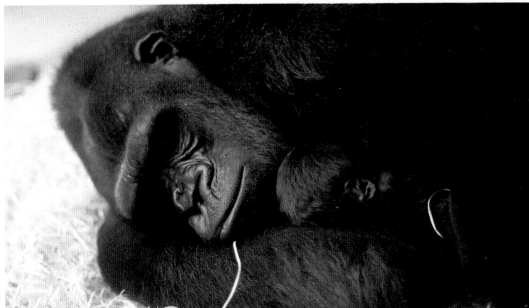

As the baby grows and becomes more active, it will begin to take its place in the group. By the time the young gorilla is one year old, it will join the other youngsters in play. But its mother will always be nearby to provide comfort and protection.

Left: *As young gorillas grow, they become more active and curious. This mother gorilla seems to be puzzled about what to do with her restless baby.*

Opposite: *When a young gorilla is a year old, it is ready to join the group and play with other gorillas. Because this youngster lives in a zoo, it may not have any playmates.*

A young gorilla rides on its mother's back.

Playing is important in the development of young gorillas. As they run, climb, and swing in the trees, they exercise their muscles and become stronger. By playing together, the young also learn how to get along with other members of the group.

Young gorillas playing near the silverback of the group. The young seem to enjoy being near their giant father.

Some of the activities of young gorillas seem very much like the games played by human children. Gorillas have versions of Tag, Follow the Leader, and King of the Mountain. They seem to enjoy these "games" as much as their human relatives do.

As the young gorillas grow older, they will eventually give up these rowdy games. They continue to develop more rapidly than humans (although much slower than many other animals). By the time a female gorilla is about 7 years old, she is an adult and can have young of her own. Male gorillas don't complete their development until they are about 10.

Young female gorillas, like their brothers, usually leave the family group when they become adults. They may join other groups or form partnerships with single males. Female gorillas do not usually live alone.

When young males leave the family group, they may live by themselves for a few years. Single males may also join together to form temporary **bachelor groups**. But they are always looking for females so that they can start their own families.

The destruction of their forest home has brought mountain gorillas close to extinction.

For thousands of years, mountain gorillas lived quietly and successfully in their forest home. But now that safe home is threatened, and the gorillas have come very close to extinction. In the early 1990s, there were only about 400 mountain gorillas left in Africa. Lowland gorillas are more numerous, although their numbers are also shrinking.

Like many animals around the world, mountain gorillas are in danger because of the actions of people. The area in central Africa where they live is also home to many humans. Populations are growing rapidly, and every day, more and more people need more and more food.

To provide food, large parts of the rain forest where gorillas once lived have been cut down or burned. The land is being used for raising crops or grazing cattle. As their forest has disappeared, mountain gorillas have been pushed into smaller and smaller areas.

The national parks in Zaire and Rwanda were established to protect mountain gorillas and their remaining territory. But even in these places, the gorillas are not completely safe.

Mountain gorillas are sometimes injured by wire snares set to trap antelopes.

People enter the parks illegally for many reasons. Some come to cut down trees for firewood. Others want to trap small antelopes that live in the forest. Gorillas sometimes get their hands or feet caught in the antelope traps and are severely injured.

Even worse, some people come to the parks to capture or kill gorillas. They may be looking for a baby gorilla to sell to a zoo. In capturing a baby, the hunters often end up killing all the other members of the group.

Sometimes hunters kill adult gorillas for their body parts. Hard as it is to believe, some tourists in Africa want to buy the head or hand of a gorilla as a souvenir. Every year, some gorillas are killed so that people can have these terrible trophies.

The countries of Zaire and Rwanda are doing their best to protect mountain gorillas. Gamekeepers and rangers patrol the national parks daily. They search for people who are cutting wood illegally or setting traps. The rangers also keep an eye out for hunters, who are usually armed with guns and other weapons. The work is dangerous, and sometimes park officials are killed trying to keep the gorillas safe.

These rangers are holding spears, guns, axes, and saws taken from hunters and other people who entered a park illegally. When such people invade their territory, gorillas are put in danger.

Because Rwanda and Zaire are very poor countries, they cannot afford to spend a lot of money on the protection of mountain gorillas. But people all over the world are helping to make sure that the gorillas survive.

In many different countries, organizations have been formed to assist in this work. Their members collect money to pay for equipment used by the park rangers in Zaire and Rwanda.

The international organizations also sponsor research projects to study mountain gorillas. From this research, we may learn more about how to protect the gorillas and keep them from extinction. We cannot afford to let these close relatives disappear from our world.

GLOSSARY

ape: a member of the primate group made up of gorillas, chimpanzees, orangutans, and gibbons. Gibbons are called *lesser apes* because they are smaller than the three other members of the group, known as *great apes.* All apes have barrel-shaped chests and front limbs that are longer than the hind limbs.

bachelor group: a group of young male gorillas that have left their family groups. The "bachelors" may stay together until they can find females and start their own groups.

groom: to clean or arrange fur using the fingers. Primates like chimpanzees and monkeys spend many hours grooming each other. Among gorillas, grooming is not so common. Mothers groom their young to keep them clean. Sometimes the silverback will also groom a young gorilla.

mammals: animals that feed their young with milk produced by the female's body. All primates are mammals.

nest: a platform of branches on which gorillas sleep. A gorilla makes a nest by bending down low tree branches and tucking them under its body. The animal may also add branches broken off of trees.

primates: mammals that belong to the scientific order Primates. The group includes small animals such as lemurs and bush babies, as well as monkeys, apes, and human beings. Primates have varied physical characteristics, but most have hands and feet that are capable of grasping. Some primates, particularly apes and humans, are also noted for their large brains.

silverback: an adult male gorilla that is the leader of a gorilla group. The name comes from the silvery hair that develops on a male gorilla's back when he is about 11 years old.

Organizations that help gorillas

The Mountain Gorilla Project
African Wildlife Foundation
1717 Massachusetts Avenue NW
Washington, D.C. 20036

The Digit Fund
45 Inverness Drive East
Englewood, California 80112

World Wildlife Fund
1255 23rd Street NW
Washington, D.C. 20037

Flora and Fauna Preservation Society
Zoological Society
Regents Park
London NW1 4RY
England

Frankfurt Zoological Society
Alfred-Brehm-Platz 16
D-6000 Frankfurt/Main
Germany

INDEX

ABOUT THE AUTHORS

Paul H. Bürgel (left) and **Manfred Hartwig** (right) are very much involved in the international effort to protect gorillas. They have made many trips to Africa to study and photograph mountain gorillas in their forest home. In 1982, Paul Bürgel founded an organization called *Berggorilla Patenschaft* (Mountain Gorilla Foundation), which supplies money and equipment to the national parks of Zaire and Rwanda. Manfred Hartwig has also been active in this organization, which in 1991 extended its goals to include saving the rain forest in Africa and other parts of the world. In their native Germany, both Paul and Manfred write articles and give lectures and slide shows telling people about gorillas. They also supply photographs of gorillas and other animals for use in books and magazines.